America Bound

America Bound

An Epic for Our Time

All best wishes,

David Radavich

David Radavich

2007

Plain View Press
P. O. 42255
Austin, TX 78704

plainviewpress.net
sbright1@austin.rr.com
1-512-440-7139

Cover art: "Southwest Impression" by Stephen Dudek.

Acknowledgment: "Great Flood" appeared previously in *Big Muddy*. The author wishes to thank the editors and readers of that publication.

Contents

Invocation

The story of a nation's rise
in global prominence

let me speak
without hypocrisy

its rich veins, its blood
lines spreading out,

listening to the voices
of those who lived simply

for themselves
and others

in the
heartland of their history,

soil and memory
and desire,

without making
headlines or being elected

or even being heard
except within these lyric pages.

Foundations

Rock Face

It seems so old—
and of another time. Cool

to the touch, barely
alive, reliable

and yet it knows the heat
of passion pouring

over all crevices,

memory coming out in the sun,
lizards perhaps, scurrying,

tufts of desert
grass idly willowing.

Inside is another story:
ruptures, one age against another,

creatures who breathed time
and now rock,

vertebrae, leaf fronds
frozen inside this sepulchre

that sometimes slides open
to reveal the circulatory tissues

we all share, moving
much slower

than our human centuries.

Somehow that hardness calls out:

Make me into weapons, grind
against knives, use
my solidity for houses

or throwing against oppressors.

You only think
I don't know pain,

suffering, memory, remorse.

Why do you imagine I'm so resolute?

Only endurance, says the poet,
keeps life in place.

Here, sit on the ledge,
look out across that ridge
and see insubstantiality of air,
how clouds push

casually over cactus
never caught in spines,

rattlesnakes know where to loll

and time stops
life a thief
without an opinion.

Birth Unto Nation

From the national beginnings,
a dance of opposites.

Hamilton and Adams versus
Jefferson and Madison, federalists
and democrats,

national law and states' rights,
rich bankers versus small farmers,

slave-owners and the man-purchased,
property versus people,
center opposite the margins,

those who vote against
the voted against, or not allowed
to ever vote.

Men over women.

Homeless without mandate.

Community law against personal appetite.

Sometimes one, sometimes the other
takes the lead, calls the music.

Sometimes a war:
Civil Rights, Women's Suffrage,
abortion for the unfortunately pregnant.

The right to bear automatic arms
and call it hunting.

Who pays taxes, who benefits, who decides?

Will the populace turn unruly?
Will the moneyed groin stifle dissent,
take over governing?

The side-step never ends,
only the pirouette changes, song

adapts rhythm
when fatigue sets in.

The CEO and factory worker,
service associate, wrapped in each other's

electoral arms.

If the tune is fortunate,
a nation of paradox conjoins.

Dollar Almighty

Originally it was not omnipotent.

Currency like any other,
pre-Civil War, before global conflagration

and corporations became persons
under the law.

Gradually, free speech became selling
and everywhere is marketplace,

even the soul,
eyes looking at trees.

It has been a history of God
overtaking gods, overturning shrines,

spreading monotheism.

Yet every god becomes eventually jealous,
division inflames and worship leads

to idolatry, distortion.

Every buck loses horns,
deliquesces in plutonial half-lives
with longing repercussions.

Odd how this coin,
this piece of paper can make

me superior to you,

entitle me to health, house,
and happiness among the less abled.

Such power adheres to few,
yet the cards get reshuffled every

now and then in
this game of transactions.

Whatever breath is left
that cannot be priced or sold
retains a sinuous strength

beyond ideology, colonialism,
armies stationed across the globe,

resistant as cloves
in teeth

tasting of loss.

Our Town

Troy, USA resembles most parts
of the realm—no relative to the mythic

home except occasionally,
in fund-raising.

Lots of signage, truck-stops
on the highway, women's groups who try

to bring culture, their version of
beauty to the benighted.

Nothing much heroic happens.

Not that we don't feel strongly about
mostly individual tragedies that
people snigger about.

Victims usually leave town.

No gift-horses here, certainly
not large wooden ones, but the mascot
of the high school is a mustang—

that wannabe Western connection,
running free on the plains.

Troy is what the overblown
has turned into: ordinary, undisturbing.

What happens to cauldrons
of catharsis when the mortgage
comes due, insurance,

teen prom-dresses, hot wheels,
materialism that flattens out every
difference and leads to

transaction.

Average is good, what we expect
and feel comfortable with.

Everyone is basically nice,
like ourselves, unpuzzling, uncovered.

We do have a few eccentrics.

But they're no more visible than
unpainted houses, corner cemetery-stones
that have been turned over by teens
during Halloween parties.

Troy is, well, beyond heroism.

When inhabitants want to feel proud
but know better and no one
criticizes what cannot be changed.

Social organizations are dying,
fast-food establishments serve Sunday
dinner, catering will go
wherever you want for a price.

Losing the week's football game
is cause for misery—or a drunken gathering
before the parents get home.

There are layers here
an anthropologist would love—
no one has dug that up, no one dares,
despite the rhetoric.

"Try the unexpected in Troy."

That's a laugh: Truth is, nothing's unexpected,
and if it did appear suddenly, wouldn't be American,
something alien and foreign.

Time is a train we get on without stations.

Strangers sometimes climb on
bringing odd baskets, accents, baggage,

but we know the direction we're heading without
looking. Just glance out that window:

Nothing worth the focus of eyes,
only fields blooming and a sun we wish

would stay forever, but it won't and that's just
the way life is—this is Troy, after all.

A boy's name with a vague
remembering we sometimes claim.

Chronicle

Our town was not always so peaceful.

In the early days, quarrels between settlers,
real estate scams, then the fool's rush

for California gold.

During the Civil War,
supporters of South and North
squared off over loyalties, finally settled
with a blanketing of dead

at the Old Courthouse.

The Progressive Era was no picnic
for workers, while the Depression begged

hand-outs at every back door.

Civil Rights showed up at the local
diner, fathers and sons stopped speaking
over hair and serving in Nam.

Women gave up quilting
for business and peace committees.

I wasn't there, but you can see
the remnants—bullets in stone, statues,
fringed newspaper files,

a few older women leading tours
through the history museum.

Most of that is forgotten now:
movies and fast food, cars that scream,

amnesia of the entertained

seeking deliverance from the self.

Our trees still shake their heads
like school marms over the city parks,

canopies hang as careful
eyelids over the stony Town Square.

There's not much blinking
where I come from.

In the early days, evangelists
at rivered tent revivals, presidents by rail

came and went with the weather.

Locals gathered like sheaves
to listen and whisper.

Now TVs blink their blue
isolation inside these dark walls

that time has built
between us and ourselves.

Complexion

The make-up of our town
has changed a lot.

After the first settlements from North,
South, and East, adventurers heading westward
with fresh pioneering supplies,

early last century
came the shoe factory

with employees of many tiers.

Since then another factory
is owned by a magnate in Indonesia,
jobs have gone "Third World,"
and the population

is mostly
rainbow for the heartland.

From my perspective, a good thing
to get some contrast in the social bouquet,
makes life more interesting,

but of course not everyone agrees.

Some prefer whitebread German,
Anglo, whatever they thought was original
whenever that was.

Of course, original was Native
American, most of them driven out,
starved off, diseased into

extinction

so this land could be "ours."

Now you can find names
of all persuasions—Indian from India,
Croatian, Japanese, Colombian

in our phone book
of domestic hooked lives.

No one much notices
strangers like us who move into new homes
around the corner and begin mowing.

Truth is, neighbors don't pay
much real attention to each other.

The question is
whether your yard's neat,
the marigolds or daffodils growing,
mail doesn't pile up too long.

Kids play Renegade in the street
with anyone who agrees to be Other.

I don't see much harm in that.

The murders we know
are mostly girlfriends, ex-lovers,
parents who deny their children a way
out of prison.

The voices who join in
are not the same
as those who spin out
to the wider world cracked for glory.

In our town,
wildflowers keep changing
in the breeze every week or two

like crazed calendars.

Great Flood

The Great Flood of '93
was Mesopotamian in its majesty.

Wide like testaments,
powerful as an arced scythe,
enough to make us all
wobble on
our sacred stilts.

No one could stand in its way,
not even mayors or corrupt preachers.

I still picture it clearly:
frozen as far as the naked eye
can see, hellish ice

against the sun except
it was summer and unnatural,

trees poking out like carrots,
cubes—or corners of cubes—arched
for air above the waters,

birds neither flying nor returning
but shivering alone, in branches hardly

green and still as death
at the end of a symphony when
the conductor puts down the baton

and no clapping—

Just so nature held its breath

Each bridge stood mired in liquid lapping
at its thighs, like the mythic giant

struggling to free himself
and walk away in the moonlit night,

only trapped and sinking,
busy with thought and traffic
going nowhere.

Prometheus in chains.

Whole towns were moved atop
bluffs nearby, new streets,
new town halls, new boxcar houses,

at least one town outright died,
residents thrown out like birdshot
on a dizzy afternoon.

Heroism didn't seem enough:

Water kept coming, and more
coming, no one knew from where—rain

had stopped long since
but the cisterns up north kept

emptying their blue arteries
on our heads, our dull minds like

sullen stone.

One man deliberately broke
our makeshift levee—Cain against
his own race,

so there were calls for execution
scrawled across the tops
of shrinking walls.

And then afterwards everywhere
mud and débris, heartless
excrement swamping the spirit

before it could even get out of bed
and start scrubbing again,

crops dead as denial,
animals confused, discouraged.

Life will never be quite
the same. Oh, yes, continue, green
up again, throw out vegetation,

but the world washed
and muddied itself beyond

anything we knew or will know again:

Relentless against
history, trespass, signaling

a time to come when
humans will no longer be welcome,

the rest of life
will continue calling from
skeletons of trees

hiding in darkest soil

waiting for rescue

Voices
of the People

Stage One

Ellie

It felt like a spring of—opportunity.

Lord knows, we suffered enough
before the war. Everyone did—lay-offs,
shortages, doing without, one hand behind
our backs, managing to cope.

We were no different
from folks across the tracks.

I always hated sponging off my parents—
though they never said a word.
What could they say?
Any day it could be us scratching
at that back door like dogs, asking for food.

The war almost seemed like a Godsend.
All that activity, industry again.
Asia seemed so exotic.

I didn't ask John what he saw
that he didn't tell me, who he had fun with.

Better not to know. If he came home
on his own feet, I'd be happy.

Hope kept me going all those years,
letters sometimes in a bundle
like a small baby. Felt like my birthday!

I never thought he'd die over there.
Never could believe to myself he would give
himself up to the Philippines, though so many did.

John seemed to be charmed—
'least back then.

That's why I let him sweep me up
that first high school dance—proud as a flower.

But when he came home, something
had changed. A piece missing somehow.
Big as a blue ocean.

It wasn't shrapnel, or a leg.
Something invisible, clawing inside
and he couldn't *say*.

But we were together again,
and Joey was born, it all seemed hopeful,
almost triumphant.

Victory at war,
and victory in our home.

That's what it felt like.

The labor was awful—hours and hours—
but even that seemed tolerable,
my little war effort.

Joey was so cute!

And John left his ghost for a while over there
on some beach, where it belonged.

It was a jubilant time.
He even took me dancing again.

Joey seemed to have the best of us both,
in his face, in his crawling around.

Always so curious about the world.
Everything new and exciting.

I could hardly hold him,
he was so restless to get moving.

The whole world seemed to open up
as never before, places I never even heard of.

And John would give me
that sad smile maybe things were
turning again, death was not
clinging to his blood anymore,

those awful snakes and leeches weren't
holding him to the ground, writhing.

For a while it felt like a new party
happening, and maybe I was the hostess.

Thaddeus

I'm not goin' back.

I been over there—during the war,
marchin' through eastern France, Germany,
all in a group. It was mostly

watching and waiting,
not much actual warfare, wearin'
us down to our skeleton.

I seen it. I was there.

And ain't no goin' back. No, sir.

Celie got the worst of it, doing without
here at home, worryin' all her days. Never
did get some o' my letters.

I came home, I was a changed man.

I seen it over there, how
they do and don't do, throwing flowers
over our head. Now is different.

I don't want my wife and child
put up with any more of what went before.

Uh-nh. I grew up with that.
Livin' in fear, thinkin' you was less
than a man. No, sir.

Ain't goin' back to that road.

My son, it's gonna be a new ballgame.
He's gonna hear pride singing

in my house.

The world out there—can't
control that, what the white cats
do who chain up everything.

But my house is sacred.
My friends. We can create
that place where we live in dignity.

Yes, we can.

We didn't get treated like
this here in France.

My Sterling is gonna grow up
believin' in himself, get
an education,

make all of us tall—
my mama who sewed herself blind
for white folks may never

see that day,
but she will know,

she will know in her soul
he made something good for himself.

That's our legacy
we're livin' down here.

I got that much thinkin' across
those European fields.

This is a changed world here, a new world,
and we gotta grab it, make it do us
our turn for a change,

startin' with this house,
this street.

My son

is gonna see different
trees and mountains out there,

his eyes gonna *survey*,

his legs gonna walk across
straight and proud.

He's gonna *arrive*.

Cindy

I don't see what's so wrong with this town.

Most people are happy—those
that want to be—crime isn't that big,
not that many girls get pregnant
without knowing the father.

Nobody's that poor.

School's no more boring
than most.

And I like the parks.

Joe and I go out sometimes
and sit all afternoon under the trees,
talking and swinging.

He says it helps him. Certainly helps me.
All those leaves fluttering so easy.

'Course not everyone fits in.

Dave runs around in his own head
like some scientist maybe,

Joe acts desperate to get away,
but that's his family, his father most
of all, not the town.

Drinking does
eat away at people.

I might feel that way too,
but my parents aren't off-the-wall
or that abusive,

they always encourage
and support me.

They'd kill me if I got pregnant!

But who'd ever want to?

Joe always calls me his best friend
in the world, his confidante,

even with all those other girls
clawing after the All-American slugger,

wanting him in their pants,
curled around their little high-gloss fingers,

Joe always comes back to me.
Says he feels safe.

But what about me?

I'm the one forced to always listen,
to show patient understanding.

It gets so hard sometimes!

I'm not your dating type—but still,
it feels sometimes like a prison.

But that's not the town.
The town's just fine. It's me.

I don't know what I can grow up to be
except a house-wife or teacher.

And either of those would be fine,
or nursing, but I need a *reason*,

someone to care for.

But that sounds melodramatic.

Really, things are pretty good right now.
The economy is thriving.

Flowers are
all starting to bloom.

It's just

Joe doesn't know I exist.
To him I'm an echo.

A place that's boring and comfortable
and never threatens to go away.

Dave

I never did belong here.

It wasn't a matter of hating
or anything—I just never fit in,
even in childhood.

The wrong genes,
the wrong predilections.

Troy is all about sports, especially
football and baseball. Autumn games
and spring and summer games,

everyone looks forward
and cheers.

Life sits on bleachers
and feels briefly meaningful.

Joe was made for that world—All-American
in both national sports, perfect spirit
of this town in its mirror.

I, on the other hand,
couldn't even see my own face.

Glasses didn't fit, I couldn't spot
the damn ball coming at me,

always got beaten
up like a sandbag or doll.

So naturally I dug into books
and hid myself in a circus of words—
which made everything worse.

But by that time
I no longer cared. At least

I won all the good scholarships.

I did go out in nature a lot. Roamed
in forests, waded in streams,
climbed up trees—

but all by myself.
Noone to bother me there.

Joe and Mike got me back good
one time in the cemetery.

It was dark as sin,
I was sitting there alone
moping at the foot of a maple

when all of a sudden this booming voice
comes out of the tombstone—

scared me to death!

I ran like a rabbit, no feet
on the ground, and then heard
their cackling behind me
all the way home.

Of course it was Joe and Mike.

Yet oddly enough, Joe and I got along
in our way—hard to imagine, star quarterback
and his book-worm friend,

but he said he respected my intellect—
I think he genuinely did—and I helped him

through a number of scrapes,
mostly math.

Spring prom was a nightmare
for someone like me.

I couldn't even ask anyone to go—
why put yourself through that charade?

I can't blame anyone but myself.
It's the wrong planet for
people like me.

Troy is about performing
your manhood, competing, warfare,
picking your side,
and never admitting defeat.

I started below zero,
so that didn't work.

Oh, my parents loved me in their way,
and I am grateful, but what can
they do with a square peg

in a town with all round corners?

Anyone who thinks, who challenges,
has edges and never fits in.

So of course my
realm lay in the mind

like a monk.

John

Where do we all go from here?

During the Depression we all struggled
as best we could, hand to mouth,
we knew where we were,
like pigs in a chute.

Now America has won the wars,
in Japan and Europe—I was there, I saw it

firsthand—the new age
of pre-eminence has begun.

I suppose it should be a golden age,
the ascendance of democracy.

Don't get me wrong.
I believe that's a good thing,
a decent thing.

We had to fight, and we had to win.
The world was watching us.

It's just—I don't know where
I belong in the picture.

When the fighting ended, I was still
in the Philippines—sick as a dog
I can tell you, but alive.

I could almost hear the two bombs
going off in my head—pure imagination,
given I was so far away,
but real in my ears just the same.

I have killed people.
I have seen their legs and arms
go flying over the hill,

beyond the palm fronds,
beyond those damn creeping vines.

How can I live with that?

Granted, this was war and such
actions are necessary.

Many of my comrades,
those I knew somewhat and those I
didn't know at all, I saw shrivel

like sucked-out animals
along the road,

or exploded like balloons with
green camouflage tatters trickling down.

A few of us—Chuck, Art, Snookie—
made it back to the States,
but for what? All scattered geographically.

How do we talk about body parts?

The nation won a great victory,
no one wants to hear nightmares.

Ellie's a good woman,
I felt proud as a president
when she gave birth

to my first, my only son,
the reward for all my absences.

Nobody's at fault—that's the way
history unfolds, America strides over

the world like a Colossus
and I am here now,

in a small town along the river
in the middle of America

having my flashbacks
that nobody understands, nobody
wants to believe

and the smallness of it all
will never measure

up to that great movie, that weird
cauldron of life I was acting
in like an extra,

nothing will seem important
ever again, like

my pin has been pulled
from the grenade of my life

and everyone is celebrating the return
of normalcy, the nation's mushrooming power.

Joe

Being a hero is so hard.

I feel like everyone has wrapped
up all their anxieties and frustrations
and put them onto me,

every touchdown I score,
every home-run I hit is somehow

part of a great cosmic victory—
not just for my parents, but for the town,
the state, even the nation,

afterglow of the war
fought by the greatest generation.

It's like performing my life,
pretending to be someone's god

not myself.

Don't get me wrong.
I like to win as much as the next guy.

I work hard, I listen to Coach,
I fight to get better.

People say I'm good-looking,
girls fawn over me, want to get in
my pants, I could get

any of a hundred women
in my high school to go with

me to prom.

Only Cindy listens to me
as an equal.

That's a problem most males would *love*,
they'd steal my jock-strap
if they could and wear it themselves.

Dave always shakes his head.

Some of it's my dad—
the war-hero come home,
forcing his frustrations into Little League
and now lately he doesn't even
attend games,

he can't take it anymore,
he's busy drinking himself to his grave.

I don't know why I knocked over
those gravestones.

Dave yelled at me to stop,
I just couldn't. Something inside me

just overwhelmed. I know
it didn't make sense afterward.

Thank god the authorities didn't find out.
Everyone protected me.
I could've been in terrible trouble.

I guess, as long as I score
enough points, the city is saved,
the school prospers.

But what does that mean,
the most points?

Who's keeping score, ultimately?

I feel like I'm living someone's dream,

icon of a generation
expected to win every time.

Success like that
scares me—

What if I get off track? What if
I fall down a hole, or have
a mass break-down?

I feel like my body is a huge battlefield
where every warrior has a stake,

my mind, my feelings
aren't relevant, just put on

a helmet and score like a maniac.

Then bow to applause.

Stage Two

Mike

I never thought I'd find myself here.

When I graduated high school
and got drafted into the military,
I thought Adventure, See the World,

give me some training
and time to sort myself out.

Boot camp was hell—everybody
knows that, it's no surprise.

But then the real zinger—Southeast Asia.

Vietnam sorta snuck up on
people, but now everyone knows,
it's a huge fight, dividing the country.

Actually being
here is beyond belief.

Not even my parents comprehend.

Part of the U.S. mission around the globe,
never sleeping, mechanical eyes
seeing everywhere.

Kinda creepy, in a way.

The locals look exotic, like alien
creatures in a film.

Base food is, well, base,
but the prices are real cheap.

It's definitely hot. Hotter
than anywhere I've been. And humid.

But your body gets used to it.
Turn to liquids, citrus,
tomatoes, salads.

Learn to savor the sweat, kinda.

Almost like it's sexy. A sort of dance
with your own body fluids.

Definitely a long way from middle America!

I haven't been here that long—
mostly work detail thus far, no real
skirmishes, but I'm sure

there'll be bust-ups
once the Cong locate us.

I'm not that afraid, though. We have
the best guns, best trained men.

Noises here are weird.

Especially at night. Creatures
cackling or cawing, sometimes whistling

or knocking. You always
feel surrounded.

And that moon—so direct,
like it's spying on your every move.

Hard to tell who's Enemy
or just a mammal hunting food.

It's different, I'll say that.

And I'm real glad Cindy writes me
almost every day. She used
to be Joe's girlfriend,

but she says no, and he's off
somewhere anyway, so the landscape's
clear for us mortals

down here.

I just hope I don't get sent
home in a box. Doesn't seem *that* wild.

Communists don't have our
range of equipment.

And democracy's all on our side.

Maureen

The conflict seems so silly.

I get up in the morning,
look at myself in the mirror,
and say, "What are they afraid of?"

Ever since I was a little girl
I knew I had a calling. I heard
voices in my head

the way others hear songs.

I felt as if God was speaking
to me directly,

issuing His challenge.

So I went to Sunday School
every week, read my confirmation
Bible cover to cover,

I was an ideal postulant.

But guess what?
Girls couldn't be acolytes.
Women could never be priests.

When I asked why, they always said,
the apostles were all men, Jesus
chose men, not women

to be around,
to preach the gospel.

And I would say, that was normal
then, men and women didn't
mix like they do now,

but that doesn't mean females
don't have spiritual gifts.

"Of course not," they would answer.
"Just different gifts."

And besides, I would continue,
"What about Mary and Martha, the first
to see Jesus resurrected,
the first to spread the good news?"

And then they'd say, read Paul:
Women are supposed to be subservient.

But Paul's not Jesus, I protested;
Jesus would never say that.

Well, the long and short
of it is, I made it through seminary—

not without sacrifice, not
without huge loans
and some men hell-bent
to throw every obstacle they could
in my way (though to be fair, other men
cheered me on, often in shadow)—

and here I am.

For years I've sung in choir
and helped with the soup-kitchen,

but the time finally came
when I said to myself,

God wants me to minister,
to share the good news and sacraments.

I don't regret the struggle,
and I don't regret being an outcast.

Finally some women had to break through,
and I thank the Good Lord
He allowed me to be in the vanguard.

Oh, it's still not easy.
In a small town like this,
some folks just up and leave—
both women and men—

they *will not* take communion
from the hands of a woman,

no matter how blessed she may be.

Others adapt to the change,
while still others embrace our quest
for wholeness and inclusion.

I don't see myself as a martyr or revolutionary.

I am a servant of God, sharing my gifts.

A town like Troy
buries many wounds.

To all who approach this table,
I say: Kneel and be reborn.

Cindy

My heart was broken when I heard.

Mike's unit came under a mortar attack,
several men were killed,
Joe lost his leg in the explosion.

A black friend
was blinded by shrapnel.

Thank God Mike made it out
with just cuts and bruises and called me
immediately he was okay.

I feel sick.

I could hardly teach
my class all day.

I know war is dangerous,
but that brings it straight home.

Stab to the heart.

I still haven't processed the whole tragedy.

Joe will never walk again normally.
Thank God he will walk and
wasn't hurt worse,

but still—the star quarterback
will never again chase after his dreams.

It just makes me cry—

though I know it doesn't do
a bit of good this far away.

And life goes on here like
nothing's wrong, economy is good,
everyone obsessed about buying that new
house or car, getting a make-over,
winning the sweepstakes.

Buy, buy, buy. That's the American way.

It all seems so shallow
when you think of friends

dying in some jungle
in a country they don't know
fighting a battle they don't understand.

I guess that's why people prefer
not to know. Too painful.

Shopping offers a kind of pain-killer escape.

I'm the same way. A new dress
makes me feel less alone, somebody
loves me or could love.

Thank God Mike writes me
every few days. He is so sweet!
Who would've thought he'd
be interested in me?

He talks about marriage, but I'm not
sure he'll still like me once he comes home.

War distorts all your mirrors.

Thank God for the kids every day.

28 is too many to cope with—I struggle
every morning just to balance my coffee-cup,
let alone gather my brain for the march
to the classroom—but their faces

are always so eager, they hug life
and won't let go, they run everywhere
and won't sit down and the world seems so
new and fun to them. It's infectious!

I can't help loving them, even
when I am exhausted. I would be
totally empty otherwise.

And just now, their hands in the air
waving madly, "Miss Pierce!, Miss Pierce!,"

bring me away from
death and dismemberment.

Only a while, but it helps.
Not even my parents comprehend.

I can't stand to be by myself any more.
I just tear up. I need somebody
to hug, to lean on.

This town, you can't
cry without causing a scene.

Dave

Why is my life either tragedy or farce?

At the same time! You decide.

My parents threw me out—
I was too weird even for them.

But that's okay. They are tax-paying,
law-abiding citizens, they believe in values
and morals and all that good stuff.

Even though I did get straight A's.

That never was enough.
How did this worthless boy ever get
thrust out of your trusty loins?

Don't ask me.

That's a genetic question
only you know the right answer to.

You have to look to your *own*
conscience for that.

Was Mom secretly unfaithful
with a circus-master? Best not to ask.

And then this latest charade.

Joe's father—after a long,
unrelenting bout of the bottle,

shades of Falstaff with his red nose—
after a long, ignominious battle

with his closest friend, booze,
gave up the ghost, bit the dust, deceased.

Joe, of course, was nowhere
to be found, having checked out.

Shades of the days in high school
when Karen and Cindy and I stood outside
at the homecoming prom

and this decidedly inebriated toper
jumped out of black bushes
and scared us to death

asking for Joe.

Right in front of the gym,
with the school-colored bunting.

Really bad taste.

But of course Joe was gone.

Anyway, this latest funeral was either
tragedy or farce. Take your pick.

It was hot as blazes,
the trees even were drooping
in memoriam.

Poor Mrs. Skinner didn't even want
to come—it was her husband who kicked
off, but never mind.

Almost nobody came, except
Cindy and me, and we had to prop
up the grieving widow

the whole time—even had
to drive to her house and force
her to the cemetery.

This is the same cemetery,
mind you, where Joe years before
had overturned so many headstones—

till I threw a tantrum
and made them both stop.

That same cemetery.

Of course it started to rain—
which did cool things off a bit—
and the female minister
who never knew

John droned on
about his stellar war record.

So now all the elms were drenched
with sorrow, and we were crying too, mostly
for ourselves and our lot in life,

and then walking back
to our car, Mrs. Skinner was hugging
and clinging to me, calling me

her true son—the same
guy who, not many days before,
was labeled a degenerate by his own family,

that same son
with a new mother

grieving over both lost husband—
such as he used to be and was—and son—
and I the interim replacement.

All too weird, even for me.
And Cindy, bless her heart, steady
as a rock, I don't know

how she does it,
God will smile on her someday.

As for me, it seemed perfect:
Drama of the dispossessed, the misplaced
healer slash griever in time of need.

The parentless child
parenting.

Can't get better irony
than that. Not in real life.

Perfect twentieth-century tragicomedy
à la Pirandello, right here in Troy.

Ellie

I don't understand what happened.

I was a good wife and mother. Always.
I made hot dinners every night—
if they came home.

And even if they didn't. Hoping.

I made Joey eat his peas and carrots
growing up. And oh, he hated it.

But I told him, "No pain, no gain.
No championship without suffering."

So he endured. Became
in fact strong and handsome.

What they call a specimen.

I wouldn't have cared if he hadn't been
All-American, but I *was* proud.

I helped him become that.

But John—nothing could help
those nightmares. Nothing I ever did
could have turned him away

from his alcohol.

I always kept a good house—
best on our street. And I never
had an affair—though I could have.

I still looked decent
in those days.

But somehow it all went wrong.
Not sudden. Slow, like
a drip down a sink.

John couldn't keep a job—
the war-hero story didn't wash
any more, and so we struggled with

bills and I had to sew
all our clothes.

Joey was a good boy—I'm sure
he still is—but he did manage to get
into trouble. Scrapes here,
petty squabbles there.

He was high-spirited, as we used to say.

And I didn't mind.
He was questing and questioning,
and who doesn't want that?

But then he went to Vietnam
and quit writing. Everything I hear
now is second-hand.

And then John

one day was found
beside the railroad tracks—

hadn't been home in two weeks.

And I'm supposed to hold
up my head, pretend everything
is okay, when something

inside me has died,
something clutches me
like lead
pulling down.

Joe didn't show his face at the funeral.

But you know what's worse?
I heard afterward he was already
in town, released from the military,
and didn't even visit his mother!

I hear he's lost a leg, too.
But he hasn't told me himself,
hasn't called.

And now I don't know

what to do. John's combat pension
is pretty much useless—not enough to live
on—and I'm not getting younger.

Everyone at church smiles
and says, "Amen," but what do they
know? A woman without means.

A world moving fast
and furious into—what? The end
of the American promise?

I feel like
I'm walking in water—
no, drowning. Hardly moving.

Can't even see
a shore.

And I've done nothing wrong!
Oh, I've committed as many sins
as the next person,

but not to deserve this.

I tried to be loving and giving
to my family. I cooked and cleaned
and nurtured and forgave.

Time and again.

And here I am—
like a rag doll thrown down.

Sterling

It all seems so ironic now.

In college, I was totally out there.
And I do mean *out there*.

Any demonstration within a hundred miles,
I was there, carrying a sign, screaming.

Black Power, all that jazz.

It felt good, it felt *real good*.
And I believed.

Whitey, The System, they were
about to go

the way of the dinosaur.

My daddy said, "Why don't you prepare
for a real job—law, medicine, even accounting?
I didn't survive the Good War for
no sociology shit."

Black Studies he always spat out
with open scorn.

But that's where it was,
the action, the freedom, the *energy*.

And it was a good place to be—
in those days. Nothing at all wrong
with majorin' in sociology.

Only no jobs.

Reality hit the Big Fan.

So I signed up, innocent as
the proverbial babe. I couldn't have
been thinking—ticket to what?

As it turned out,
the jungles of Vietnam.

Lord, I thought Alabama was hot!
Felt at first like the oven
of Satan himself—

only humid, with the air
clawin' over you with tongs.

But the setting wasn't so bad overall,
sweating, crawlin' around, pretendin' to be
accomplishin' something, till

Boom! that shell hit
and everything went black.

Black as night.

An' I'm not talkin' African
skin black, which is mostly brown
anyway, 'least in my case,

I'm talkin' black
as everlasting absence
of any light, sun or moon,

blind as Oedipus
in—where was it?—Thebes.

Joe was beside me with his leg blown
off, laughing like a maniac, "I'll never play
baseball again, I'll never play
baseball again,"

almost like he was glad
to be rid of the American pastime.

But I looked out
and saw nothing more

than the end of my favorite life,
the life I had been so busy acting in—

no more Civil Rights,
no more upping The System,

just feeling my life
ooze out like the lost soul
I always was,

prisoner

of the Old South
not yet crawlin' to the New.

As the man said, sockets dripping
in tainted blood, "I was blind,
but now I see."

I see in myself
a fool of the first order

who believed we could really
change The System, make it help

the poor, the damaged,

the folks with the dark skin
who suffered so much and will *never*

get their justice
without some serious blood.

Man, was I a babe!
Innocent and so blind—

and now I stare at the world,
I look at everybody through the heart
of myself and see it

clear as a shell

break open like a flower

Stage Three

Joe

Wow! The country has changed so much.

I came back in the autumn—
leaves were floating down from
the trees, everything

turning brown,

just like every year—
only it all seemed different.

I'd only been gone for three years,
but now I'm walking on
a wooden leg,

still a little stiff,
not used to old Charlie,
as I call him,

people looking at me strange.

"Just feel lucky you didn't get killed,"
they say to me. Like

I'm supposed to feel grateful.

The country's in deep
recession, so there's a seriousness,
more desperation, in the air.

So I go to the unemployment office
in the weather-beaten high-rise,
ask to fill out the papers,
the woman says,

"You're not eligible."

"What do you mean, I'm not eligible?
I gave up my leg for my country."

"Your leg," she says.
I said, "Sure. Look. Here.
Wooden from the knee all the way down."

"Wow," she says. "I wouldn't've
known from seeing."

"I did my time in Nam.
So I'm entitled."

"No, you're not," she said. "Only
if you've already had an approved job."

"Approved job!," I said.
By this time I was almost yelling.
"What have you given for your country?"

"I pay my taxes," she says.
"Bet you haven't paid *all* your taxes,"
I said back. Silence.

"See?," I said.
"You're working here
at this shit job, and I'm sitting
home unemployed with my body
given for Uncle Sam."

"Sir, I don't appreciate
that kind of language," she says.

"Ma'am, I don't appreciate
your kind of attitude."

The upshot was, with my skills—
playing ball—all I could

get would be minimum
wage, a clerk or some factory.

Wow. A little card
with phone and address

was all I came back
to, all that creeping through
jungle under fire,

all that screaming
in your ear in the dark night,
exploding just when you thought
everything was peaceful.

What a crock.

They oughta do better
than that. I put my life out

there

like a gift.

Bob

Young people are so spoiled these days.

They're used to privilege—
even when they don't have nothin'.

It's an attitude: Entitlement.

Not like in my day,
when you scraped and was grateful
for every scrap you could get.

No, sir. They got no concept
'bout the world, how
things operate down low.

So this new guy marches in—
Mike, I think his name is—eyes big
as saucers, like he's never
seen a warehouse,

he comes in
and says, "So what's the deal?"
"What deal you talkin' 'bout?," I said.

"You fill out these papers,
and you take their papers, then
you shred their papers
and put the new ones in the file."

Don't ask questions, I tol' him,
and you'll be a happy man.

"What do you mean, don't
ask questions? You're my mentor."

I said, "Look, kid. I been here a long time,
the system works. Trust me."

"We doing something
illegal here?"

Legal, schmegal. It's capitalism
we're doin' here. You don't have to
know all the details.

Somebody makes a profit
stealin' from somebody else,

some sucker agrees
to it, got yourself a deal.

"What are those trucks really carrying?"

You don't wanna know.

But the guy doesn't let up; he's a real bulldog,
this one. Fresh back from some war.

"Do the drivers know what
they're hauling?"

"Some do, some don't,"
I tell him. "Those can afford to, know.

Others got a wife and kids,
a tough mortgage."

"Wow," he says.
He uses that word a lot.
Like he's just discovered this world
is not so much beauty and light
as he once thought.

I sympathize.

I guess I'm just jaded.

Comes from marriage breaking,
living alone, too many years working

makes a man hard in his soul.

But he's a good kid,
basically. I try to help him out best I can.

Wish I could lie to him better.

The bosses—what can I say?—
don't like hearin' the truth either,
so I keep my nose clean,

know what I mean.

It's not bad around here.
Fumes don't get to you 'less you let 'em.

And the guys on the floor
are great. They know what's goin'
down, and they stick together.

Kind of a family
in the end.

Karen

I don't believe in redemption.

Not any more.
I'm too old; have too
many wrinkles to show for my life.

Actually, I'm not *that* old,
but I *feel* like it. Two failed marriages
will *roast* your self-confidence.

Thank god I didn't have kids.
I'm stupid, but I'm not bonkers.

Though I'd like to someday.

Working at the trust
office doesn't cut a *slice*.

Don't meet eligible men,
life stalls in a boring routine,
paychecks and utilities, no room

for hope, so you try personal
ads, intermediaries,
nothing seems to pan out.

So don't blame me for the nightclubs—
not my choice. Desperation.

After a long, hard week
and waking up every morning
totally alone.

Well, guess what?

Last night I see this guy
from behind near the bar, looked
kinda familiar, like I knew this profile

but somehow different—

it was Joe, from our
high school days back in Troy!

The quarterback
who took me to the prom.

Old war years,
long ago and far away.

I asked him what he was doing
so far from home, in the city, he said,
"Working at a bakery,"

"Oh," I said,
and sat in silence, listenin'
to the music beat
sky-scrapers in my head.

What do you tell
about ten years you wasted?

"Let's dance!," I said finally.
"You used to kill the dance-floor."

But he clammed up tight,
hemmed and hawed and stalled
till I almost got angry,

then told me
he'd lost a leg in Vietnam.

"Oh, my god!," I said.

"I didn't know anyone over
there personally."

"That's the common perception."

Then he showed me the leg
so I'd believe. "I'm not
from Missouri; you don't need to prove."

His eyes narrowed:
"I know where you're from."

"Wow," I said. "You've changed."

"So have you."
"Is it that obvious?"

After that he backed off
faster'n a snakebite,

"No, you look good. Honest.
Just older, that's all."

"And somewhat wiser—I hope."
(I was reaching.)

"Yeah," he said. "We all hope for redemption."

"Wow," I said. "That's the very word
I've not been believing."

"What's to believe?
Life is something you do battle
with and stumble home with scars."

"Tell me about it."

Then he looked at me
with those wounded eyes—

damn, he looks good!, I thought—
granted, I'm feeling desperate, but damn!

That face

did something to my self-esteem
right then and there.

"What d'ya say I cook you up
some breakfast," I asked.
"Where is that?"

"My place," I said.
"I make a mean omelet."

"I bet you do," he said slyly.
"No dancing."

"Agreed. No dancing—with the feet."

And then he leaned into me
with his eyes more than this close,

"I can do redemption," he says,
"I see it on your face."

And off I went
like a lit firecracker.

Gerald

I'm doing the best I can.

Ellie's a wounded woman,
almost an invalid, I would say,

but it's not like I've
wandered through life
without

my own mess-ups.

Dropping out of school, getting
in fights, going back, quitting this job
and that, getting divorced

from a woman
I never should have married.

But, I'm in contact with my kids,
I made enough to live on.

I try to help Ellie
best I can
based on my experience.

We met at the post office,
of all places! I was just buying
stamps when this

pitiful, lost woman
was struggling with her purse
and seemed to need me.

I know that sounds sick.

But we met a few times, something
flowed back and forth like

a switch turned on.

And it's not as if
we're not every one of us
wounded in this world.

Modern life is brutal, that's for sure.

I try to get her interested
in art, music, theatre, to open
up emotionally

to the good life.

But she still blames men
for all that went wrong in her life—
husband absconded, son
a hero who was

supposed to fix everything.

Can't blame her
feeling disappointed.

I'm not sure she loves me.
I'm not sure she can love anyone
anymore. How can a shell

get new insides?

But I truly want to take care
of her—if she'll let me.

It's not altruism. I have my own
needs, how I see myself,
enough money,

and I'm not getting younger.

I can visit, I can decorate, bring
some light to her place,
open up, create

air and life
in a house that knew pain.

I can help her garden,
I can take out the weekly garbage.

I want to ease her dying days,
and that'll ease mine.

Every human being deserves that,
every last one.

Sterling

Life is so crazy sometimes.

And when you're blind like me,
it's a circus of sound.

There we were, all gathered
for Karen and Joe's big wedding—

I flew in, lots of folks from Troy
made the trek over, music

was all set up, flowers,
even a minister who could cope
with these crazy people—

everything you could imagine,
plus a crisp fall day with that bite
in the air that's refreshing,

felt kinda good
on your face—

only no bride showed up!

Folks were to-ing and fro-ing,
in and out, Jackie stayed with me outside
along with Cindy and Mike, but Joe
was all aflutter like a schoolgirl,
jitter-buggin' everywhere,

at one point the organist came out
and said, "Should I postpone the prelude?,"
and nobody was sure,

then the pastor came out
and looked like she aged some
this afternoon,

truly a huge carnival,

and all through this Joe ran
in and out, yelling, "She blew me off,
I know she did," and I tried

telling him, "No,
prob'ly she's just late,"

and he'd answer like a wounded
animal, *Not this late,*

and Cindy would say—
Mike let her do the talkin'—
Cindy would say, "I'm sure there's
a good reason and she'll be here soon,"

and Joe would moan out,
"I *know* the reason—she doesn't
love me any more," finally

I said, " Hey, man. You're a soldier!
You can handle this. Stay cool."

But Joe just whined,
"This is worse than Vietnam!"

I never seen such carryin's-on.

Jackie whispered to me on the sly,
"I'm glad ours wasn't this much charade,"

and in-between we carried on
this disquisition about the break-up
of the American family,

how the fabric of the nation
is unraveling, divorce and what-not,
all very learned shit,

and how no one cares
about anybody any more,
just themselves,

the pastor came out
a few more times, and just
when Joe'd turned
almost totally insane

I heard a taxi pull up and I knew:
Help is on the way!

Karen got out in a mess
and ran to her bridegroom,
who was a worse mess, crying
and apologizin',

it turns out her ex-husband
Jeff had found out she was re-marryin',
and he came to her apartment
and started abusing

her so she couldn't come,
but she managed to climb out
and call a cab.

All very heavy stuff.

In the process, of course, her dress
got torn and she had bruises but nobody
cared we were so happy.

I never seen such a teary wedding,
but in the end it all happened,
including Joe's mother,

who was kinda in a daze,
but we did it, we tripped them
lovebirds off on their life adventure

and I'm not sorry
I couldn't see it, 'cause
I heard more'n I needed to

and true love
is sometimes better

not looked at too closely.

I know, 'cause I've been there
myself, it's best you keep your head
screwed on tight.

Juggler can't take his eyes off
one second

or it all falls down.

Maria

Sometimes you just have to laugh.

No other way.

A requirement in my line
of work, helping AIDS patients

die with dignity
in their penultimate days.

I like that word "penultimate"—
my favorite since college.

One of those words
that sticks with you,
walks with you alongside.

Nursing—how can I tell it?—is
in crisis, and yet, human
beings will always

need to be cared for.

Some a lot easier than others.

That's why I appreciate Dave so much.
Always lively, always quick with
a word to make us laugh.

Gorgeous with language.
He loves my "penultimate."

You can hear him cackling clear
down the hall. All the patients love
him, those who can hear.

Certainly makes my day.

Last week this guy comes in
with one of those huge balloon
bouquets, the kind with streamers
and metallic colors,

walking kinda gingerly,
like he was hiding something,

and surprised
Dave in his sleep.

They talked about old
times together, overturning

gravestones, silly childhood pranks.

Must have shared
a wholesome upbringing
back there in the middle West.

They were catching up
when all of a sudden the guy freaks—
Dave starts talking of dying,
planning his funeral.

Dave jokes about having him
sing with his horrible voice, picking out
music, chorus girls in white, etc.,

and the guy suddenly
turns stone cold and says,

"you're not gonna die."

And Dave laughs like he always
does, like a mockingbird,

"I hope so; otherwise,
it'll be a pointless funeral."

But the guy says no,
it can't happen, he can't
accept death,

it's not Dave's reality,
it's nothing he can endorse.

We get a lot of that
here: Denial.

Americans don't believe
in endings—only adventure,
new beginnings, not wrapping up.

But the results are clear:
Sooner or later,
you gotta get off that stage.

Gather up
your harvest and go.

People ask me, how do you stand
it, being around all that dying?

Actually, I kinda like it.

No more time for dishonesty,
people become real,
they have time to think,

to regret, to get rid of all
that baggage they been carrying.

'Course that can get real
ugly sometimes, and you want
to step aside and let it all

blow up
out in the desert.

But I treasure the good ones.

Dave's in that category.
I consider him a friend.

I'll definitely
go to his funeral.

I wanna hear the hosannas!

Stage Four

Karen

Everything comes to an end someday.

Even if it's premature.

We just buried Joe's mother, Ellie,
well before her time—she just gave up
somehow. Never recovered
from Joe's departure

and her husband's demise.

On one level, I don't blame her.
But it's sad.

Hardly anyone came to the funeral.
Gerald was there—bless him.
Loyal to the end.

But he couldn't bring her back.
Prob'ly nobody could.

I wanted Joey to go to the service—
he's seven now, that's old enough, I think,
but Joe said no, so we hired
a baby-sitter.

I can understand that he's
traumatized about funerals, but
you need to introduce kids to death
gradually, and naturally.

It'll only be worse later.
Oh, well.

It was a gorgeous, crisp winter
day, with everything sparking under
the sun. Afterward

we flew home
and just sat on a bench
in the park, talking about life.

Then suddenly this balloon-vendor
walks up—in December!—

asks if we need
a lift in life,

and Joe tells him, "Hey, I make
balloons for a living, and a lot better
than these," so the guy said,

"Okay, okay, have a nice day,"
and slunk away.

I wanted to go by then—
even though we were wrapped
in our winter coats,

wind still biting at the ears—

when these two punks
showed up, wanted our wallets.

I was scared to death
and told Joe to hand them over,

but no, of course Joe wouldn't do that,
they got in a fight and he fell

hard against the bench,
cutting his head.

I screamed and wanted
to call an ambulance, but he said
he'd be okay. In the end,

they did throw
back the family pictures
he wanted, and the empty leather.

I was a mess during all this,
but Joe started laughing—just
couldn't stop,

and I said, "What?!"

"We're gonna make it."

"What do you mean, make it?" I asked.

"You see those ducks out there?"

(Ducks were all around
and in the pond, and we'd been
feeding them breadcrumbs.)

"Those are greedy little buggers.
And they know we got food in our hands.
They know we'll feed them."

"They don't know for sure.
We might not have breadcrumbs,
or we might not share them."

"They know. They're American
entrepreneurs. They go after what
they want. It's capitalism."

I had never heard him like this.

"But we're gonna make it."

"I hope so," I said.

"I *know* it." And he kept
throwing, throwing out those crumbs
oh so smoothly,

like the baseball-player
he used to be.

I asked him, "Joe, are you happy?"

He looked at me
with welling eyes and said,

"I can't believe I've come this far.

A miracle."

Gloria

If only I knew then what I now know.

Life is too short
to learn all the lessons
you need.

Dave died all alone—

I guess his friends were gathered,
but his parents rejected him.

His parents!

The ones who brought him
into the world, who nurtured him.

Herb was adamantly
opposed I should go to him
and apologize.

He said we were right
not to support a degenerate,

I said, but what is a degenerate?
An unloving father, who doesn't claim
his own flesh and blood

in time of trial?

You can imagine how that
went over.

But I didn't stand up.
I let him bully me into silence.

I knew it was wrong.
I didn't follow my heart, what
I understood deep inside.

We never met his partner
in those last years. I'm so glad
he had somebody

to brighten his days with.

Somebody to get up to for breakfast
and drink coffee, somebody who cares
you're alive, an assuaging

warmth in bed.

Now I don't have that either.

And I'm robbed of my son.

I can't even go to his grave!

Actually, I think he was cremated,
but anyway, what good would that do,
in this horrid shell of a house?

The pictures are cold ghosts
to me now. The walls glare at
a trespassing stranger.

Maybe I could find
his manuscripts somehow—

uncover who he really was that I didn't
know. Maybe save him again
if I edited his life,

took it to a publisher.

I'm willing to do that. It's the least
I could do to reclaim my son.

I think he was brilliant
underneath it all.

I shouldn't say underneath.
I mean, we didn't see, Herb and I,
the world, he died unknown.

I don't have much else to do.
I'm well-off, free of all bonds, Herb
left me well provided for.

I don't even miss him
that much, the chapter's over,
I did what I had to do after the war

and made a good home.

Life's different now.

I haven't used the china in years.
We don't do dinner parties, people don't
gather like that any more,

we're on our own
like snow-men, I guess.

I can only read and reconstruct
what was—my only son I never saw
for years—in words,

a few worn photographs.

Maybe Patrick will give me
access if I beg enough, if he can
forgive me as a mother

on Dave's behalf.

I've never begged before—
not for a long time—I should have
begged with Herb.

But what did I know then,
life can be taken away

so fast

you can't mend it,
can't say good-bye?

Samantha

I can't *stand* it—not any more.

Oh, my parents think
they're so liberal and all that,

they've seen the world,
but they don't even have a *clue*.

The world's falling apart all around
and they have no answers.
None.

And this is a small town
better than most.

I mean, it's not their fault,
but they don't understand my
generation *at all.*

Who cares about school?
I mean, for one thing the system
sucks, you don't learn
anything useful—

'specially at our cute
little campus with uniforms,
where we're programmed for success.

Don't you love that?

Your well-meaning parents,
Cindy and Mike, in the manicured
house with the hydrangeas
and wind-chimes,

pay oodles of money
to a school that turns out
cookie-cutter students who know
how to fill out college-entrance exams
and get into

"the best schools"—
the best schools being, of course,
where the wealthy hobnob

and prepare to
get even wealthier while

the world blows up in discontent
and appalling social inequity.

Well, I don't buy any of it.

And you can imagine how my parents
freaked when I dyed my hair
and spiked it.

The nose-ring
really got them—pierced
them right to the heart, which,
in a way, was the point,

to break through
that tortoise-shell reality
of theirs,

but it's *my* body
to do what I want with,

I told them, you've only got one,
so you need to make it
beautiful.

"That's not beautiful,
that's ugly," they said dismissively.

"I beg to differ," I said,
and stormed out. Haven't been back
since, except to collect my things.

I'm not putting up
with that! I know my own
heart, what I need.

I'll make it somehow,
pimping if I have to, modeling,
odd jobs here or there.

Right now
I'm staying with friends.

They don't mind.
They know the world's cruel
and the country's falling to pieces,

and parents are, well,
clueless to cope with anything

except switching on
cable TV—

that remote control
is the closest thing Dad
has to any grasp of his life.

I don't mean
to be mean—they're nice people,

not really objectionable,
not Mussolini or anything,

but they're never
really *out there*—know

what I mean?

Charles

I guess I'm my papa's revenge.

All those marches and demonstrations
in the Civil Rights Movement,
all those angry speeches

have come to me

and he feels betrayed.

I don't blame him. That's his world
and all. But I'm not turning
back on civil rights.

I'm takin' it to a new level.

See, it's history, it was necessary,
but that's not *my* life.

The story now is making money.

You're not a person 'less you have it.
So I'm gonna get it, and
I'm gonna call out their dance.

Black people are never gonna triumph
'less they become entrepreneurs—

I know it sounds crazy,
but all those hip gang-lords
are only businessmen

plyin' their trade
in the 'hood.

Folks don't like that kinda
business, but that's what it is—
trade in America's weakness, what
people need to *pretend*

everything's gonna be okay.

The dark underbelly
of the American dream.

I don't wanna go there.
I want a better life, where I'm
the *chief* and the *referee*.

That's why I got my MBA.

Daddy and momma were appalled
at my economic priorities.

Well, it's not just greed.
It's common sense in a nation
that measures your manhood in dollars.

Native Americans woulda been
better off if they opened businesses
everywhere—not just casinos

but dance-clubs with feathers
and beads, hunting boutiques you can
go to and pretend you're wild,

Indians don't get the program,
but you have to grab, and grab hard

if you hope to survive.

People don't wanna hear that stuff.
I don't blame them; it's hard
as rock to absorb.

But I want to be the one
with the hammer, the carpenter
they talk about.

With all those extra hours
and networking, I'm not sure
I can manage a family.

Doesn't mix
with getting ahead.

Now'days only losers have kids,
and no one else cares about helping
bambinos. I don't agree,

I think it's wrong, but I didn't
make the rules, I'm jus' playin' the game.

Daddy claims
I have lost my soul.

But I wouldn't call it that.
I'd call it making the soul pay

for itself, pay its own way.

I'm *tired* o' begging,
and nobody bleeds his heart
to give me a damn thing.

I don't see anybody wanting
to help a black man—just wanta
lock me up, throw out

the key,
forget I exist.

I'm not buyin' into *that* scenario.

No, sir. I'm gonna make
me some money and buy up

my freedom,
one little dollar at a time.

That's *my* sacrifice
for the cause.

Mike

I don't recognize this life anymore.

It's all changed—nothing
I grew up with is still whole,

institutions are corrupt, or bankrupt,
or both—or they're simply
dead and gone

like extinct species.

Science gone to the rats.

Even our daughter hates us—
and many other people's children—
for reasons that baffle me.

I don't think it's fair.

We did our best; provided every amenity.
We wanted our child to be prepared,
which she was. At least

we thought so.

I guess not. Not in her mind.

Everyone's turned so selfish and brutal.
Even here in Troy. Callous about
the suffering of others.

It feels cold and wintry,
like people have lost their warmth.

Lord save us from showing
any weakness!—

We might get run over
by the stampede.

It's like we're not human if we're not
buying every minute—little consumatrons
they can program

to spend money on cue.

I realize this makes me sound
old and crabby. I'm not *that* old,

not able to retire yet—
though I'd like to, get out
of the ratrace,

Cindy feels the same way about
teaching, how they overload her with
too many students to handle

and then threaten
lay-offs.

Not a world I understand.

I think of that ultra-violent twentieth century,
with its world wars and multiple
genocides, and I almost

cast a longing, lingering look behind.

Friends of ours fantasize about
leaving for Canada or Central America—
isn't that a laugh?—

where buddies of mine
got blown up or ripped open
in the '80s—

You won't find me
moving anyplace near!

But where to go
that's safe from violence,
hypocrisy, torture, lust after greed?—

your body becomes almost
a punishment

instead of a temple.

I do have trouble sleeping now.
I wake up with nightmares, thinking
of houses being stormed

in small villages,
families not comprehending
how America could come to stand
for torture in the name

of Democracy.

Not the country I grew up
in or want to be.

But I'm alone now—
with Cindy and few friends—

in this outdated cell
of idealism.

Oh, well. Such was the lot
of most humans in history, who
had no influence on

their country or what
it could or would become.

I wanted ours to be different!
A haven for the hungry, the homeless,
the harassed, those driven

from other shores.

Now we're the driven,
and we don't even know
which shore.

Joey

History doesn't get made in a teacup.

You either roll over the other
guy, or get rolled yourself.

Torture or be tortured.

Those are the rules of war,
so you can't be pretty and take prisoners.

An Arab comes up to you,
you shoot, and ask questions later.

I'm not sayin' it's right,
I'm not sayin' it's good.

But you have to protect yourself;
the guy could be camouflaging a bomb.

And in any case, it's one
less soldier, one less insurgent

for the other side.

Look, I'm not the ringmaster here.
Most of human history,
this is the norm.

I don't have to love it,
but sure as hell can't sit home and
twirl my thumbs like a girl

and pretend there's no problem.

No, sir. We're here
to get things done, help

these people set up their own country.
Simple as that.

Somebody's gotta do it.

That's America's role in the world,
forging democracy for
all freedom-loving people.

And everyone loves freedom—
'cept those in power, who hate losing
control, who rig elections
and maintain

one-party government
through corruption and pay-offs.

My parents aren't too wild
about my being here.

They didn't actually oppose it—
after all, my dad lost his leg in combat,
so he's one to talk, but

they thought there
wasn't enough justification.

I say, the justification
is, we're here, we're trying to

make democracy where
there wasn't one,

we need to civilize these people
best we can so the world can be safe.

I'm not a knee-jerk military man.

I hate mess-halls
and tromping around
with these monster guns—

hell, I feel kinda sorry
for the little ones and the women,
who look up at you all sad in the eyes
and pleading like

they don't understand a word.

I feel for them inside.

But you can't let that get
to you or disorient your objectives.

I do hope my tour o' duty
won't be extended.

I walk out alive, I can go
home, maybe get a girlfriend
and have kids.

I'd prefer not to limp
like my dad, but hey, you take
what you get and leave all the decor.

That's my philosophy,
and I don't think I'm all
that unusual.

I'm proud of my country,
and proud of myself for putting
up with trash that woulda

buried anyone else,
made him bitter or sorry.

I pray God
keep me upbeat

and confident against
all odds. Like a good soldier

marching
in the host of heaven.

Epilogues

Questions

I hear the voices of America,
voices of the people

from every region, every condition:

Will the sun rise on our dreams
or set on our sorrows?

Will the unfortunate—poor,
mindless, sick, enchained, underage—
find their haven?

Will Justice take off
her blindfold, raise her voice
against tyranny?

Will trees lash their bodies together
and walk off leaving no history?

Will greed take up residence
in our garbage dumps and chide
us like magpies?

Will night bring up our sins
and let them escape as shadows
in the morning mist?

Will we remember all
who have lost, the sacrificed
who gave us their eyes?

Will we dance over the graves
of our ancestors, chanting their names?

Will we know when we are free
and rejoice in the fray?

Will we listen when the owl calls
us to the barricades?

Will we rescue our souls
before the flood of the covenant?

Tell me, my people, all
you have to say, what you hear
in the small, flickering light,

what leaves can be
steeped together,

what craft
can ferry the future,

point us somewhere home.

Memento

Like the leaves of Bernini's laurel
in Rome—impossibly light, miraculous

yet astonishingly real, a triumph
of art over the world

we see die and long to escape:

Even so, hard as words on a page,
black upon white, unalterable, a species

of remaining miraculous,

this aching reaches
for salvation, pursued, transformed

by the searching, bare fingers clutching
stone flesh even as the dry tears

die earthward, into air

we are pulled
as pursuing gods-to-be—

Male and female,
bound and fleeing, turned

and turning as a people who chase
ourselves into rock—

Unless the hammer
shatters or bombs obliterate

to no more than
a memory of verbs

or eyes mar
all loving beyond

what the body can become
in a world of clamoring,

the ideal lives on

in the clang of chisel on self,

raw physics of centuries
opening

veins of desire.

End Of Empire

Every empire dies in over-reaching,
dissipation, then collapse.

Degradation of the natural.

Disaster on land and sea,
starvation, drowning.

Stones tumbling like eyeballs.

A season turns,
the Earth floats onward

in its starry space.

Back again to plant and rock.

A new empire
emerges with glorious

shoots, full of flame
and flagrance, the confident self

seeking to save
an old mind that has built

much now broken.

It is the story
of rising and falling,

tides in a single
man or woman's sojourn

among rocks and trees
fed by rivers
not of their making.

Air that spreads
of its own accord.

It is a story
nearing its stormy end.

Welcome the new life

Welcome death and rebirth

Welcome the sweeping
scythe

into worlds to come

About the Author

David Radavich is the author of *Slain Species* (Court Poetry Press, London), *By the Way: Poems over the Years* (Buttonwood, 1998), and *Greatest Hits* (Pudding House, 2000), along with several chapbooks. In addition to a wide range of poems in journals and anthologies, he has published a full-length comedy, *Nevertheless . . .*, and four short dramas. His plays have been produced across the U.S., including five Off-Off-Broadway, as well as in Europe. Radavich has given poetry readings in such far-flung locations as Egypt, Greece, Iceland, and Scotland and enjoys directing and performing in dramatic readings. His essays, both scholarly and informal, have appeared in journals varying from *American Drama* to *U.S. News & World Report*. *America Bound* weaves the author's love of both poetry and drama into a larger national narrative.